Exeter's Royal Visitors
from Roman times to the present

Exeter's Royal Visitors
from Roman times to the present

By
Tony Lethbridge

ALI-KAT Publications

Ali-Kat Publications
'Tresco'
6 Lower Kings Avenue
Exeter EX4 6JT
England

By the same author
The Story of Exeter Speedway Volume I.
  The Non-League Years 1929–1945

ISBN 0 9515149 1 1

Phototypesetting by 'The Studio', Exeter, Devon.
Printed and bound by BPCC Wheatons Ltd., Exeter, Devon.

Contents

For Christine with love.

ACKNOWLEDGEMENTS

My thanks go to all the people who have helped me produce this book. In particular Brian Matthews for taking the photographs, Len Dawkins for his splendid drawings, and the staff at The Studio for putting the whole thing together. My colleagues at the Westcountry Studies Library, Ian Maxted, Margaret Westcott, Tony Rowse and Peter Waite, have as always been very helpful and extremely patient. My wife Christine has sorted out most of the problems, made endless cups of coffee, and done the proof reading, while my parents Ted and Pat, and uncle, Dick, have once again been brave enough to back the project.

BIBLIOGRAPHY

Eugene A. Andriette, Devon and Exeter in the Civil War, David & Charles, 1971.
John Gibley, Royal Visits to Exeter, 1863.
W. G. Hoskins, Devon and its People, Wheatons 1959.
W. G. Hoskins, Two Thousand Years in Exeter, James Townsend, 1960.
Robert Newton, Eighteenth Century Exeter, University of Exeter, 1984.
T. J. Northy, Illustrated Popular History of Exeter, 1886.
Rev. George Oliver, The History of the City of Exeter, 1861.
Nicholas Orme, Exeter Cathedral as it was 1050–1550, Devon Books, 1986.

AD 49 ARVIRAGUS

The first recorded visit of a royal personage to the city of Exeter comes from the mists of time. The story originated from the medieval chronicler, Geoffrey of Monmouth, but post World War II excavations have confirmed that the Romans occupied the Exeter area circa AD 50.

Geoffrey relates that in AD 49 a Roman force under Vespasian was sent by the Emperor Claudius to subdue the South West of Britain. Vespasian and his Second Legion landed in Torbay, and marched to Exeter, at that time a fortified settlement overlooking the river.

For eight days Vespasian's soldiers launched continuous assaults on the earthwork defences of the settlement but failed to break through.

Meanwhile Arviragus the King of Britain, hearing of the Roman attack, marched with his army from the East to relieve the besieged city. However after a long and bloody battle, night fell without either side gaining the upper hand. Darkness forced both sides to withdraw, but the next morning Arviragus and Vespasian made peace after the Britons' queen had mediated.

Although this story may be more legend than fact Roman relics have been found which prove that the Second Legion was stationed in East Devon in the year 49.

Later that year it is also recorded that Genevissa, the daughter of the Emperor Claudius visited the now Roman held settlement.

The novelist Rosemary Sutcliffe may have adapted the legend of the battle for the opening chapter of her famous childrens' story 'The Eagle of the Ninth', part of which is set in the Roman city of Exeter, known as Isca Dumnoniorum.

The Romans occupied Exeter until the beginning of the fifth century, turning it from a fortified village into a properly laid out town complete with all the principal features such as public baths, basilica and market place. The Romans first built new defences in the form of an earth bank five feet high and twenty feet wide, but in the year 200 this was replaced by a wall. This wall would later form the outline of the medieval city wall much of which can still be seen today.

AD 632 PENDA, KING OF MERCIA

The Dark Ages which followed the departure of the Romans produced another royal legend. Matthew of Westminster, a medieval chronicler records that in 632 Exeter was besieged by Penda, King of Mercia.

The legend relates that Edwin, the Saxon King of Northumbria, had been at war for some time with Cadwallin or Cadwallo, one of the last kings of the Britons, whose realm included Cornwall and West Devon as well as Wales. Cadwallo was finally driven from his home in Wales and took refuge in Ireland. There he attempted to reform his army in readiness for an attempt to regain his lands. But his efforts were in vain as Edwin was always on the alert, and his adviser Pellitus made it his business to keep him informed of Cadwallo's movements.

Cadwallo became so frustrated that he approached Salomon, King of Armorica, now Brittany in Northern France, for help. Salomon advised that an assassin be sent to murder Pellitus. Acting on this advice Cadwallo dispatched his nephew, Brienius, to carry out the evil deed. Brienius quickly set off for York where King Edwin held court. There dressed as a beggar, he waited outside the King's gate, as by custom food and alms were distributed to the poor.

When Pellitus, who was also the Royal Almoner, came out to distribute the alms Brienius attacked and stabbed him with his poinado, a small dagger. Amid the pressing throng it was easy for the murderer to make his escape. Eventually his travels led Brienius to Exeter where the citizens still being Britons greeted his confession with joy, and ever hopeful of seeing King Cadwallo regain his kingdom, set about putting their city in a state of readiness for his attempted return.

Meanwhile King Penda after hearing of the murder from his neighbour and countryman King Edwin, also received word that the murderer had taken refuge in Exeter. He immediately set out with his army and lay siege to the city. The citizens manfully resisted his attack and held Penda off long enough for Cadwallo to arrive on the scene where he promptly defeated Penda's army and reclaimed his kingdom.

Danish Raider.

Historians give very little credence to this legend. Records do show however that Cadwallo was a Welsh pagan king and in 633 along with Penda invaded Christian Northumbria where he slew Edwin at the Battle of Heathfield near Doncaster before ravaging Edwin's kingdom. Cadwallo was killed by King Oswald at Heavenfield near Hexham in 634.

AD 876 ALFRED THE GREAT

In the year 875 Danish invaders made a sudden attack on Exeter and having captured it spent the winter within its walls where they inflicted considerable damage and treated the inhabitants with characteristic cruelty. But in the spring King Alfred marched westwards to relieve Exeter. He met the main Danish force along the way and totally defeated it. Hearing of Alfred's victory and his imminent arrival the Danes fled from the city, but not before they had suffered the vengeance of those they had persecuted. Many fled to Dartmouth and were drowned in a great storm at sea. Others retreated to Chippenham from where they continued to harry the Saxons.

Nineteen years later the Danes again attacked Exeter, but this time the inhabitants held them off long enough for Alfred and his troops to come to the rescue. The Danes lifted the siege and escaped to their ships before he arrived although several of their vessels were captured at sea by the English fleet.

Alfred spent time in the city during which work was again undertaken to repair the damage and improve the fortifications.

AD 928 ATHELSTAN

In 918 Edward the Elder held a Wittena-gemote or general council of his chief subjects in Exeter. Seven years later Athelstan, Alfred's grandson, succeeded to the throne but the Britons in Exeter and the West refused to acknowledge him as their rightful king. Athelstan marched west with his army and drove the rebels from the city and right out of Devonshire, after

A section of the City Wall near South Street.

which the River Tamar was recognised as the boundary of the Cornish Britons.

Athelstan returned to Exeter where he rested and rebuilt the city's defences. The "huge bulwarks of earth, strengthened by stakes, and surrounded by ditches" were torn down and instead the city was surrounded by a stone wall, a mile and a half in circumference, flanked by towers and with a deep and regular fosse, or moat, around the outside.

A number of other benefits were also bestowed upon the city by Athelstan. These included the original castle at Rougemont, the re-establishment of the minster or monastery, dedicated to Saint Mary and Saint Peter, as well as the privilege of a double mint. Later Athelstan became a regular visitor to the city and on one occasion held a Wittena-gemote at which a body of laws were enacted for the protection of property, the administration of justice and the punishment of offenders.

Among Athelstan's noblemen was one Edgar, who took for his third wife Elfrida, daughter of Ordgar, Earl of Devon. Edgar was described as a man of "gigantic stature and strength". On one occasion when the King arrived at Exeter late at night and found the East Gate shut and barred, with the gatekeeper absent, this huge man unhinged the gates with the "mere force of his arms" and then kicked them open so that the King could pass through. After his death Edgar was buried at Exeter but his thigh bone was preserved at the Abbey of Tavistock until the dissolution in the sixteenth century.

Athelstan is accredited with changing the name of the city to Exancaester from which obviously Exeter is derived. Since 450 the Saxons had known it derisively as Moncton due to the large number of monks who lived locally.

1003, SWEYN, KING OF DENMARK

The threat of attacks by the Danes eased during Athelstan's reign but the weak government of Ethelred the 'Unready' became an inducement for the marauders to return. The danger was quickly realised when a Danish force appeared off Exmouth in 1001 and word rapidly reached Exeter that invaders had landed and were approaching the city. The citizens had little time to prepare their defences but when Sweyn, the Danish King and his force arrived outside the city their furious attack was withstood by the determined resistance of the defenders and the strength of the rebuilt fortifications.

The siege lasted for two months and within the walls the defenders situation became grim. But relief eventually arrived in the shape of force of Saxons from Devon, Somerset and Dorset under the command of generals Cola and Eadsig. They attacked the Danes at their camp at Pinhoe, but although the invaders repelled the attack, Sweyn withdrew to Exmouth where after burning Pinhoe, Broadclyst and other villages along the way the Danes re-embarked in their ships.

Although Ethelred fitted out a fleet to counter the Danish threat, the fleet's commander Edric, Duke of Mercia went over to the enemy taking half the ships with him. The remaining ships took shelter in the River Exe below the city.

During 1002 on the orders of Ethelred, all Danes in his kingdom

The burning of Exeter by the Danes in 1003.

13

were slaughtered. Among the victims was Gunhelda, Sweyn's sister. The following year Sweyn returned to England determined to avenge his sister and his fellow countrymen.

Sweyn advanced on Exeter, and the citizens fully aware of what would befall them if the Danes broke through put up a desperate defence. Their courage could have overcome the danger had it not been for a traitor in their midst. On 19 August 1003, the governor of the city, a Norman by the name of Hugh, let the Danes into the city and Sweyn's vengeance was terrible indeed. The city was rapidly reduced to ashes, the citizens were slaughtered in cold blood and the defences torn down. Not even Hugh the governor escaped. He was dragged away in chains by the Danes.

The destruction by Sweyn and his Danes was the greatest disaster to befall Exeter until the Blitz of 1942.

1050 EDWARD THE CONFESSOR

Sweyn's successor, Canute, attempted to atone for the cruel acts committed by his father. Canute assisted the citizens to rebuild the city's defences and a royal charter was granted to re-establish the rights and privileges of the monastery of St Mary and All Saints. Thus from the ashes arose a new city.

The Saxon monarchy was restored with the accession of Edward the Confessor and during his reign Exeter flourished. To add to the city's prestige the united Sees of Devon and Cornwall were removed, with the concurrence of Pope Leo IX, from Crediton to Exeter with its city walls.

Leofric who had shortly before been nominated for the See of Crediton thus became the first Bishop of Exeter, and King Edward attended his enthronement in person. This event took place in the Saxon minster and was a grand and elaborate affair. Leofric was conducted to his episcopal chair with the King supporting his right arm and the beautiful young Queen Editha his left. This trinity is recorded for posterity in a stone sculpture above the sedalia at the high altar of the present cathedral.

1068 WILLIAM THE CONQUEROR

In the wake of the Norman Conquest in 1066 Exeter was one of the last pockets of resistance to hold out against William the Conqueror. Having defeated King Harold at the Battle of Hastings, The Conqueror became William I of England when he was crowned in Edward the Confessor's new abbey at Westminster on Christmas Day but all of England did not immediately recognise his rule. In the east Hereward the Wake held out until 1071, but in the west resistance centred around Exeter.

King Harold's mother Gytha and her daughter, Edith, took refuge in the city where she had a fortified house, thought to have been sited in the Bartholomew St. area, and thus the resistance movement developed. The defences were repaired and others of similar loyalties were invited to join the garrison. Another cause for Exeter's refusal to accept William could also be found in his demand that an ancient tribute of £18 a year should be increased.

Whatever the reason Exeter's rebellious population could not be overlooked and early in 1068 William marched on Exeter. He sent a messenger to demand that the leading citizens should swear an oath of loyalty to him. The citizens refused and replied that "We will never swear allegiance nor admit the King within our walls, but we will pay him tribute according to ancient custom". This tribute traditionally went towards the dowrys of the queens of England.

The citizens reply was certainly not to William's liking and he angrily marched westward with a combined Norman and English army. When word reached Exeter that the King was approaching the city council sent out a deputation to meet him at his camp four miles outside the city. When they came before the King the deputation appeared to have lost their nerve and pleaded for peace. They undertook to obey his future commands and left him with a number of hostages to ensure the city's good behaviour. However their fellow citizens did not frighten so easily so when the deputation returned within the city walls and reported what had happened they were furiously disowned and their action repudiated. The rest of the population were determined to resist

15

The Normans arrive outside the walls of Exeter.

The site of the South Gate where William the Conqueror launched his attack on the city.

16

and the defences were immediately put at a state of readiness. William arrived outside the city with 500 horsemen to find the gates closed against him and the walls lined with armed men.

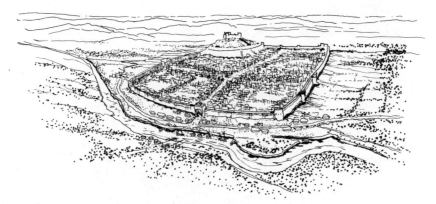

Norman Exeter.

William displayed his authority by having the eyes of one of the hostages put out. The only response this gruesome action drew from the defenders was an obscene gesture from a youth on the wall, which caused William to fly into a rage and launch his attack on the city. This confrontation probably took place outside the South Gate, at that time the main point of entry to the city.

William besieged Exeter for eighteen days. He attacked day after day and his engineers tried to undermine the defences but without success. Within the walls the suffering was very great as it was mid winter, but equally William's situation grew more and more perilous as every day that Exeter held out, the greater became the chance of the rebellion spreading throughout the South West. Several attacks resulted in severe losses for the Normans, but eventually a section of the wall suddenly collapsed offering the attackers a way into the city. This disaster for the defenders resulted in an armistice being agreed. For his part William swore a solemn oath not to harm the city, and kept his word by stationing trusted guards to prevent the rest of his troops from looting. In return the citizens agreed to a Norman garrison being stationed within the walls.

The Norman Gatehouse of Rougemont Castle.

18

Meanwhile as the Conqueror had entered the city at the end of the seize, Gytha the Saxon queen mother, her daughter, and retainers had slipped out through the Water Gate and escaped by boat down the River Exe either to Flatholm Island in the Bristol Channel or to Flanders.

While his engineers began clearing the site to start building a castle on a spot selected personally by William, the King headed off to Cornwall in the spring of 1068 to complete his conquest of the South West.

The castle was built on the volcanic hill in the northern corner of the walls and became known as Rougemont. Having secured the south west of his kingdom, William ruled with an iron will but allowed the citizens a certain amount of compromise.

1137 STEPHEN

Exeter was besieged again 59 years later during the Civil War which swept England as Stephen and Matilda fought for the throne. Matilda the last surviving child of Henry I was usurped by Stephen, his nephew, who was preferred by those in England and Normandy for whom the idea of a female ruler did not appeal, although many nobles stood by Matilda. Among these was Baldwin de Rivers, Earl of Devon, who took the Norman castle at Rougemont with his private army and fortified it and the city for the Queen. However he called on the citizens to acknowledge his authority but instead they sent to Stephen for help, and the King immediately marched on Exeter.

Baldwin de Rivers meanwhile attacked and burned part of the city before withdrawing into the castle, which was strongly garrisoned, well provisioned and had an adequate water supply from two wells.

Stephen's combined army of English and Flemish troops arrived and lay siege to the castle, where they were constantly harried by forays from within the walls under cover of darkness, and showered with arrows by the defenders on the battlements. As a counter measure wooden towers were built to give Stephen's men protection while they launched an attack on the castle with

The ditch and defences surrounding Rougemont Castle are now public gardens.

King Stephen's army lay siege to the Castle 1137.

21

seize engines which constantly hurled large stones within the walls.

In the early stages of the siege Stephen's cause was aided by the capture of a outer earthwork, which is thought to have been situated at Danes Castle, near the present fire station, which gave a fine view of the castle.

The defenders of the castle held out for three months despite Stephen's engineers continually attempting to tunnel their way under the walls.

Eventually a shortage of water forced them to surrender. Unfortunately for the garrison the supply provided by the wells was not sufficient for the large number of humans and animals sheltering within the walls. The defenders were forced to rely on a plentiful stock of wine which apart from drinking and cooking was even used to extinguish fires started by the King's troops.

When even the wine gave out de Rivers offered to surrender if Stephen spared the lives of the defenders. Although the King at first refused he later changed his mind and accepted the Earl of Devon's offer.

Stephen took no revenge on the city but contented himself with confiscating the property of Baldwin de Rivers and banishing him to Normandy as it seems that there had been a personal grudge between the two men. They later appeared to have made up their differences as de Rivers regained his title. Stephen meanwhile generously paid the canons of the cathedral compensation for the damage caused to the building by the siege.

1285 EDWARD I

The next royal visit to Exeter was brought about by a murder. In 1283 a bitter feud had developed between the Bishop of Exeter Peter Quinil and the Dean, John Pycot. The Bishop did not approve of Pycot who had gained his position by questionable methods. However Pycot was a local man and had the backing of the mayor, Alured de Porta, a powerful administrator, who had held his office for six consecutive terms starting in 1276.

28.   Ancient South Gate (Old Debtors Prison demolished I   Wor   Ser

The Southgate in the Eighteenth Century.

23

The precentor of the cathedral, Walter Lechlade, was very much the Bishop's right hand man, and as such was regarded as a threat by both the Dean and the Mayor. As the feud grew a plot was hatched to murder Lechlade, and the foul deed was carried out in the early hours of 10 November 1283.

The office of mattins was said in medieval times just after midnight, and as Lechlade left his house, the Chantry, now the Cathedral School, he was watched by one of the mayor's servants, Thomas the Leader, who hastened to the South Gate which had, by prearrangement, been left open. There Thomas sounded a horn and from the darkness crept a band of men who slipped through the gateway into the city.

Just over an hour later Lechlade left the cathedral still wearing his white vestments and, accompanied by two servants, started to walk the short distance back to his house. Just as he reached it the band of attackers struck him down. Taken by surprise his servants fled but their shrieks of terror and the death cries of Lechlade himself quickly brought the residents of the locality to the scene. They discovered the Precentor lying dead in the muddy roadway with two terrible head wounds and a broken arm and

Precentor Walter Lechlade was murdered here within yards of the Cathedral.

blood stains spreading across his vestments. The city authorities also hastily arrived and the coroner demanded that the corpse must not be moved until it had been officially viewed. However the clergy mindful of their jurisdiction over the precincts thought otherwise and an unseemly dispute ensured.

Eventually the Precentor's corpse was carried to the Charnel Chapel which stood close by the cathedral to await burial. This took place inside the cathedral before the high alter.

The murder of the Precentor had long reaching effects. In time charges were brought against the Mayor, the Dean and twenty other people. Among the accused were both clergy and laity including the vicars of Heavitree, St Leonards and Ottery St. Mary. After many delays the Bishop eventually took the matter to the King and thus Edward I, his queen, Eleanor of Castile and three of his daughters, Eleanor, Joan and Margaret arrived in the city on Saturday 22 December to spend Christmas 1285 in Exeter, the only reigning monarch ever to do so.

The Royal Family stayed in state at the Castle and it is likely that they attended the Christmas mass in the Cathedral. However the trial was the main reason for the visit and it began in the Great Hall of the Castle on Christmas Eve. Five laymen including the Mayor, Thomas the Leader and the Keeper of the South Gate were all found guilty on 28 December and sentenced to death. They were led out and hanged immediately. The clerics escaped much more lightly.

Dean Pycot and his henchmen were committed to the Bishop's prison but were soon released after purging themselves before the Bishop and a jury of twelve clerks. The Dean was however relieved of his office and retired to a monastery. The actual murderers appeared to have escaped justice.

As a result of Lechlade's murder the King gave permission for the cathedral churchyard to be surrounded by a high wall with five gates which could be closed at night when the curfew bell was rung. The tradition of ringing the Curfew still continues. The main gate was St Michael's or Broadgate. Although the gateway is long gone, it is through this entrance from the High Street that visiting dignitaries still enter the Cathedral Yard.

Edward I visited Exeter again in 1297 whilst travelling to and from Plympton where he stayed while inspecting preparations for an expedition to France.

Broadgate in the Eighteenth Century.

1345 EDWARD, THE BLACK PRINCE

Sea travel in the Middle Ages was an uncomfortable and often dangerous business but the royal ties with France and Spain meant a great deal of coming and going, especially with the advent of the Hundred Years War. The small ships of the time made it advisable to voyage between the closest points to the destination so travellers frequently travelled overland and embarked at Plymouth rather than sail down Channel if they were heading for Spain and Portugal. Therefore it followed that many royal travellers passed through Exeter.

Exeter's ancient Guildhall.

Edward, the Black Prince, the eldest son of Edward III, was a frequent user of this route. He first visited Exeter in 1345 whilst on a tour of his properties in the Duchy of Cornwall and spent four days in the city on his return journey. In May 1357 Edward passed through the city on his way back to London from Bordeaux bringing with him King John of France whom the Prince had captured at the Battle of Poitiers the previous year. Opinions vary on this story as other chroniclers contend that the royal party landed at Sandwich in Kent and travelled via Canterbury to London.

In 1362 Edward III created his son Prince of Aquitaine, and the Prince came through Exeter no less than five times as he travelled backwards and forwards to Plymouth making final preparations for his return to France in June 1363.

The Black Prince last visited Exeter in 1369. The war in France had broken out again and all was not going well for the English. Edward and his family were struck by an illness, and the Prince returned to England following the death of his eldest son. Edward landed at Plymouth in December 1370, but it was not until the following Easter that he set out for Exeter and the difficult road to London. Upon his arrival Edward was confined to bed because of his illness at the home of the mayor, but his wife, Princess Joan, the Fair Maid of Kent, and the four year old Prince Richard, later Richard II, went to the cathedral where they made an offering of five marks.

The Black Prince's sister, 13 year old Princess Joan of the Tower, broke her journey in the city on 29 January 1348 when she stayed with the Bishop, John Grandisson. Princess Joan was on her way to Bordeaux to marry Pedro the Cruel, the crown prince of Castile. But tragically soon after reaching France the Princess contracted the Black Death and died on September 2 before her marriage could take place.

Princess Joan's mother, Queen Philippa, visited Exeter in the summer of 1349. The Black Death seems to have been the reason for her visit as it is thought that she was travelling around the West of England to avoid the plague which at that time was prevalent in London.

1403 HENRY IV

The Black Prince's brother, John of Gaunt, and his second wife Constance of Castile, passed through Exeter on 16 November 1371, but it was John's son who as King Henry IV was to be the next ruling monarch to visit the city in January 1403. Following the death of his wife, Henry planned to marry Princess Joan, daughter of the King of Navarre, and travelled down to Exeter to meet her when she arrived from Falmouth after sailing across from Brittany; the voyage having taken five days due to the winter storms. The Royal couple stayed for three days from 30 January to 1 February before departing for Winchester and their wedding.

Taken from a Picture at Hampton Court, Herefordshire.   Design.et sculp.G.Vertue

Henry IV.

29

1452 HENRY VI

The arrival of Henry VI at Exeter in 1452 heralded the beginning of a series of visits by six successive ruling monarchs. The King's visit was part of a royal progress aimed to revive his flagging support in the shires. The enigmatic Henry was not a particularly popular monarch, having lost most of England's possessions in France, and failed to keep law and order. To restore public confidence the King undertook tours of the provinces in the summers of 1451 and '52. The 1452 tour was carefully planned and gave the authorities a chance to prepare for the King's arrival. Henry crossed into Devon from Dorset on 14 July and travelled towards Exeter. He approached the city on 17 July and was met at Clyst Honiton by the mayor, Hugh Germyn, and the leading citizens consisting of more than 300 knights, gentlemen and yeomen, all attired in the city livery.

The King then proceeded to Livery Dole where he was greeted at St. Clara's Chapel by the communities of the Franciscan and Domincan convents and the rural clergy who all joined in the

Livery Dole Chapel where Henry VI was greeted by the monks.

The modern approach to Southgate.

procession. The Benedictine Prior of St. Nicholas, and the Augustinian Prior of St. John's Hospital, with the parochial clergy and chaplains, awaited his majesty at the Great Cross outside the South Gate bearing two crosses and offered incense to the King when he stopped to acknowledge the cross. The mayor presented the King with the keys of the South Gate and then proceeded him into the city and up South Street which was hung with silks and tapestries, then passed the city conduit which ran with wine in the King's honour.

At Broadgate the Bishop, Edmund Lacy, accompanied by the cathedral canons and choristers, was waiting. Here the King dismounted and walked in solemn procession into the cathedral through the West Door and up to the High Altar. There he spent some time in prayer before making his offering and moving on to the Bishop's Palace where he stayed for two nights. The King held Lacy in high esteem as the elderly prelate had been with his father Henry V at the Battle of Agincourt, so his decision to stay over in the espicopal palace was a mark of that respect.

A pleasant little local folktale has it that the King was greeted

31

The commemorative plaque at Southgate.

by Lacy at St Stephen's Bow further up the High Street. Shortly before the King arrived the Bishop turned to his clergy and boasted that the King would bow to him before he bowed to the King. The Bishop waited on the inside of the Bow and when the King dismounted from his horse he had to bow his head as he walked under the arch to greet the Bishop.

Unfortunately after his spectacular entry, the King lost a certain amount of credibility with the clergy by allowing his judges to hold a court in the Bishop's Hall at which two men were sentenced to death for treason. The decision to stage the trial on church property upset the Bishop and his clergy who protested that it compromised their rights of sanctuary. To pacify his critics the King pardoned the two condemned men, but the unfortunate incident did nothing for the King's standing. Within a year Henry was suffering from mental illness and the kingdom slid into confusion and civil war.

1470 EDWARD IV

As the Wars of the Roses developed Henry was deposed and the throne seized by the Yorkist, Edward IV. On 14 April 1470 Edward arrived in Exeter in pursuit of Earl of Warwick the Kingmaker, who had previously supported his bid for power. Edward had quarrelled with Warwick, and his own brother George, Duke of Clarence, over his policy towards France. The King and his army had sought them in the north, but Warwick and Clarence accompanied by their wives fled south, passing through Exeter on their way to Dartmouth and passage in a ship out of England.

Edward and his army dashed after them covering the 290 miles from York in just eighteen days but when he reached Exeter his quarry had already evaded him. Not surprisingly the King was none too happy about this or the fact that the city had previously withstood a twelve day siege by his follower, Sir William Courtenay of Powderham, preferring instead to support the cause of the disposed Henry VI. Edward attempted to conciliate the feelings of the citizens and after being received by the Mayor and

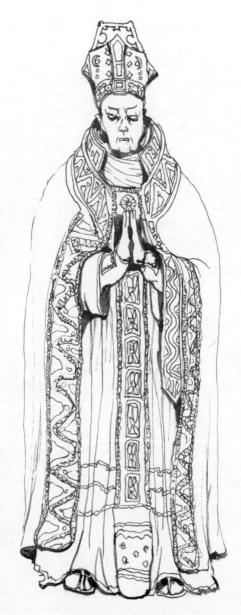

A medieval Bishop.

The world famous West front of Exeter Cathedral.

The East gate in the Eighteenth Century.

35

four hundred citizens in red gowns, accepted a gift of a purse containing one hundred nobles. The city keys and maces were also presented, then graciously returned by the King.

The next day was Palm Sunday and the King walked in the customary procession around the Cathedral Close and surrounding streets, and may even have carried the blessed palm. Bishop Stapleton's register records that the procession was extended beyond the East Gate so that all the people got a chance to see their sovereign.

After dinner on the following Tuesday Edward left the city after 'giving great thanks to the Mayor for his entertainment, as also showing himself very loving and bountiful to the people'. Before he departed the King presented his sword to the city.

The balance of power in the Wars of the Roses took another twist and four months later Warwick and Clarence came through Exeter again on their way to London where they succeeded in putting Henry VI back on the throne as Edward fled to Holland. He was not away for long and returned in the spring of the following year when he defeated Warwick at the Battle of Barnet to reclaim the crown.

In a last ditch attempt to save the throne for Henry his wife, Queen Margaret of Anjou and her son Edward, Prince of Wales, crossed the Channel from France. They landed at Weymouth and arrived in Exeter in late April 1471. From Exeter they went on to Tewkesbury where they were defeated in battle by Edward on 4 May, the Prince of Wales being killed. Shortly afterwards Henry was murdered in the Tower of London.

1483 RICHARD III

Edward IV died on 9 April 1483, and Richard claimed the throne following the disappearance of the 13 year old Edward V and his brother in the Tower. This unpopular move resulted in a spate of uprisings in the south during the autumn. Locally opposition was led by Sir Edward Courtenay and his brother Peter, then Bishop of Exeter, the Archdeacon of Exeter and the Abbot of Buckland who declared in favour of Henry, Earl of Richmond. The uprisings were unco-ordinated and Richard quickly moved to crush them.

Richard III arrives at Eastgate.

"My gracious sovereign, now in Devonshire,
As I by friends am well advertised,
Sir Edward Courtenay, and the haughty prelate,
Bishop of Exeter, his elder brother,
With many more confederates, are in arms."

Shakespeare's Richard
III act 4 sc 4.

Warning of the King's approach gave the conspirators time to escape to France, but when Richard reached Exeter on November 8 he lodged himself in the Bishop's palace, which he found extremely well provisioned. Richard and his retinue had been met at the East Gate by the Mayor, John Atwill, and the council. The Recorder, Thomas Hexte, had presented the King with a congratulatory address and a purse containing 200 nobles.

Not everybody was so pleased to see the King. His brother in law, Sir Thomas St. Leger and Thomas Rame had been found guilty of treason at Torrington and were brought to Exeter where they were executed at the Carfoix.

Atwill, the Mayor, may also have had a nasty moment whilst showing the King around his city and in particular the castle. Richard enquired of Atwill what the castle was called and when the latter replied "Rougemont", the King trembled and turned pale, for he had mistaken the name for Richmond.

"Richmond! When I was last at Exeter,
The mayor in courtesy showed me the Castle,
And called it Rougemont; at which name I started,
Because a bard of Ireland told me once,
I should not live long after I saw Richmond."

Richard III.

Although this story may have been a part of Shakespeare's effort to discredit Richard for the benefit of Tudor propaganda, the prediction certainly came true at Bosworth Field on 22 August 1485. Bishop Courtenay was present to see Richard's down fall and Richmond become Henry VII. Courtenay not only got his bishopric returned but also went on to become Bishop of Winchester and one of Henry's chief ministers.

38

The commemorative plaque at Eastgate.

The busy junction in High Street where in medieval times the carfoix stood.

1497 HENRY VII

Although Bosworth Field may have marked the end of the Wars of the Roses Henry had to crush further plots and rebellions before his kingdom was totally secured. In 1497 Perkin Warbeck, claiming to be the Duke of York who had disappeared in the Tower along with Edward V, landed at Whitsand Bay near Plymouth. He attacked Exeter around 17 September with a small force, but after burning the North Gate and breaking through at East Gate as far as Castle Lane was driven out by the defenders in a bloody counter attack. On hearing that Sir Edward Courtenay was approaching with a relieving force and that the King had offered a reward of a 1000 marks for his head, Warbeck withdrew to Taunton. However he eventually surrendered and when Henry entered Exeter on 7 October, Warbeck was with him as a prisoner.

Henry was the last medieval king to come to Exeter, and his visit was the longest ever. The King stayed at the Treasurer's house, which until 1798, stood against the north tower of the Cathedral. The King had come to thank the people for their loyalty, and also to deal with Warbeck's rebels. The ringleaders were found guilty and hanged and quartered outside the city walls in Southernhay. However, Warbeck's Cornish followers were brought before the King outside his lodgings. A large new window had been cut in the side of the house overlooking the cathedral yard where eight trees had been felled to make space for them all.

The King appeared at the window and the prisoners were drawn up before him with halters already around their necks. They fell on their knees and pleaded for mercy. After severely admonishing them the King granted their pardon, and with a great shout of 'God save the King', the prisoners threw off the halters.

Henry left the city on 3 November, but not before acknowledging his debt with the presentation of his sword and cap of maintenance, which he commanded should be carried in state before the mayor on all public occasions "from the time being forever". Henry VII's orders are, of course, still being carried out.

From an antient Limning in the Royal   Collection.   G. Vertue Inv. Sc.

Henry VII.

42

The West Gate under attack from Perkin Warbeck's rebels 1497.

The view down High Street from Eastgate. It was here that Perkin Warbeck's rebels were driven back from Castle Lane.

Southernhay where the leaders of Perkin Warbeck's rebellion were hanged, drawn and quartered.

33 EXETER.— Picture of the troublous times of 1497. Burning of the North Gate by Perkin Warbeck. September 1497.

The burning of the North Gate during the 1497 siege.

45

The Cathedral Green. The medieval treasurer's house from where Henry VII pardoned the rebels was built against the North Tower of the Cathedral itself.

46

The outline of the Treasurer's house can still be clearly seen on the
North Tower.

47

1501 CATHERINE OF ARAGON

In October 1501 a Spanish princess, Catherine of Aragon, landed at Plymouth en route to London where she would marry Prince Arthur, Henry VII's eldest son. Travelling via Tavistock, Okehampton and Crediton, Catherine broke her journey for several days in Exeter where she stayed at the Deanery. Unfortunately her stay coincided with the autumn gales and the princess's sleep was disrupted by the creaking and squeaking of the weathervane on top of the spire of the nearby St Mary Major church. A workman was dispatched to risk life and limb by climbing the spire to remove the offending instrument. Shortly after Catherine's departure on 17 October, the story goes that the workman had to repeat his ascent and replace it.

Catherine married Arthur on 14 November but the following April he died, still only fifteen years old. Subsequently Catherine married his brother, Henry VIII.

No ruling monarch visited Exeter during the sixteenth century. Although Elizabeth I is reputed to have dubbed Exeter the 'Ever Faithful' city she never came here despite it being the popular headquarters for so many of her Devon sea dogs.

The Deanery. The original St. Mary Major Church stood to the right.

48

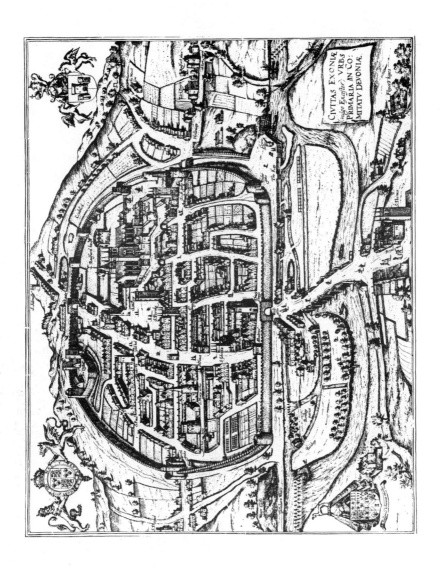

Exeter in 1618.

49

1644 CHARLES I

Exeter had to wait a further 146 years before another ruling monarch visited the city. Sadly civil war was once again the reason for the visits. The war between Charles I and his Parliament had broken out in the summer of 1642. The King raised his standard in Nottingham and after the initial encounters it became apparent that the west, south west, and the north generally remained loyal to him, while Parliament drew its main support from London, East Anglia and the south east. Obviously the situation was not black and white and areas of resistance held out against both sides.

Exeter like everywhere else had its divisions. The Dean and Chapter of the Cathedral were royalist to a man, as were the leading merchants, but the city also had its Puritan element. As the war developed a constant watch was maintained by thirty two selected citizens while supplies of food and ammunition were gathered together and stored in preparation for any situation which may arise. Six guns were mounted for the defence of the city.

During the winter of 1642 parliamentarian sympathies within

Roundheads.

Surrender of the city by parliamentary troops to Prince Maurice.

Bedford Street formerly the site of Bedford House where Charles I stayed and Princess Henrietta was born.

the city grew. Eventually all Royalists were edged out of key positions and Exeter prepared to come under attack from the Royalist forces of Sir Ralph Hopton who was by then attempting to secure the west for the king. After failing to capture Plymouth, Hopton turned his attention to Exeter reaching the outskirts towards the end of the year. By now the city was well defended and when Hopton called for it to surrender the mayor refused. Dangerously short of supplies the Royalists decided against a prolonged action and withdrew.

Throughout the winter the city's defences were further strengthened. Extra defensive ditches were dug around the walls and houses pulled down to provide the defenders with an unobstructed field of fire. Look-outs were posted at the top of St Mary Major's tower and fire precautions were undertaken.

Eventually Exeter was besieged by Sir John Berkeley and a Royalist army on 16 June 1643. During August Berkeley was reforced by Prince Maurice, the king's nephew, and eventually after an eleven week siege Exeter surrendered on 4 September.

Berkeley became governor and the city's Royalist officials were restored. A strong garrison was maintained and Exeter became the Royalist headquarters in the west.

As the main fighting in the Civil War moved away from the west the Queen, Henrietta Maria, moved to the relative safety of Exeter from threatened Oxford. She arrived on 1 May 1644, and stayed at Bedford House, the town house of the Earl of Bedford. The Russell family had acquired the site of this house in 1539, which until the dissolution of the monasteries under Henry VIII had been used by the Dominicans or Black Friars. In 1773 Bedford House was also demolished to make way for the new Georgian crescent known as Bedford Circus. This in turn was destroyed in the blitz of 1942 and is now the location of the main Post Office.

It was here in Bedford House on the morning of Sunday 16 June that the Queen gave birth to a daughter, Henrietta Anne. The little princess was christened in the cathedral on 21 July 1644 by the Chancellor, Dr. Lawrence Burnell. A new font was installed

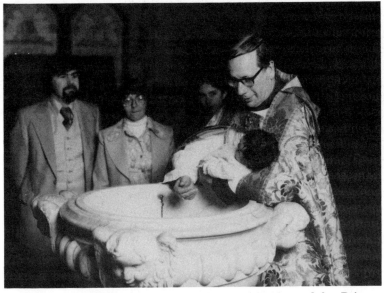

A modern christening at the Cathedral font. Was it used for Princess Henrietta's baptism? (John Clapham)

53

A DOMINICAN CONVENT
OCCUPIED THE SITE OF THIS
CIRCUS A.D. 1259.
IN 1539 IT WAS GRANTED TO
JOHN LORD RUSSELL
WHO CONVERTED IT INTO BEDFORD HOUSE
WHERE IN 1644 WAS BORN
PRINCESS HENRIETTA,
DAUGHTER OF
KING CHARLES I.
IN 1773 IT WAS REMOVED AND
THE ERECTION OF THE PRESENT
CIRCUS COMMENCED.

The commemorative plaque on the wall of the Post Office in Bedford Street.

Henrietta Maria, Queen Mother.
From an original by Van Dyck.

Her Autograph from an Original in the Poſseſsion of
John Thane.

Queen Henrietta, wife of Charles I.

King Charles I.

56

King Charles I arrives at the Guildhall.

especially for the occasion but views differ as to whether it is the one still in use today.

Meanwhile Parliamentarian troops under the command of the Earl of Essex were again advancing into the westcountry and by 5 July they had reached Tiverton. With danger threatening once more, the Queen, escorted by Prince Maurice, secretly left Exeter and made her way via Falmouth to France. She was forced to leave her baby daughter in the care of the faithful Countess of Dalkeith, and it was two years before mother and daughter were again reunited in France.

However the Royalist Army with King Charles in the vanguard was close behind Essex. While the Earl cut across country to Okehampton and on into Cornwall, the King arrived at Exeter on 26 July in company with Charles, Prince of Wales. The loyal citizens presented the King with £500 and the prince with £100. The royal party stayed at Bedford House where the King saw his baby daughter for the first time. Before leaving the next day the King knighted the mayor, Hugh Crocker, as a reward for his loyalty.

57

Charles wasted little time in continuing his pursuit of Essex, finally bringing him to battle at Lostwithiel where a decisive action resulted in victory for the Royalists.

The King stopped at Exeter again on his way back, this time staying in the city for a week, before continuing his march to Oxford. However his military success did not continue and the Civil War eventually ended with the Royalists defeat at Naseby in 1645. Charles was put on trial for treason and executed at Whitehall on 30 January 1649. Following the restoration of the monarchy in 1660, the anniversary of his execution was marked in Exeter annually by a solemn procession from the Guildhall to the Cathedral for a special service. At the head of the procession, wrapped in black mourning crepe, was carried the great sword presented to the city by Edward IV. This practice ended in 1835, and since then the sword has only been carried at memorial services for members of the Royal Family or very prominent people. At the time of writing the last such occasion for Sir Winston Churchill in 1965. Both Royal swords are kept in the Guildhall along with the other civic regalia.

1670 CHARLES II

Charles II paid a short visit to Exeter when after visiting Plymouth to inspect the new Citadel, the royal yacht was becalmed at Dartmouth and the King decided to return to London overland. Charles arrived in Exeter between seven and eight in the evening of 23 July 1670. The King stayed overnight at the Deanery where he was sumptuously entertained at the expense of the city. He was presented with £500 in gold and in return knighted the mayor, Benjamin Oliver. Charles made an early start next morning leaving at 3am to continue his journey to Wilton House near Salisbury. Charles was accompanied by the Duke of Monmouth, and his party travelled in four coaches escorted by servants on horseback. The King's early departure prevented the traditional hogshead of wine from being emptied into the great conduit at the Carfaix.

The following year the King sent, as a gift to the city, a portrait

58

of his sister Henrietta. Henrietta Anne had grown up in France in poverty with her mother, and had eventually married Phillipe, Duke of Orleans, the brother of Louis XIV, the Sun King. She had been described as the 'Fairest in all Christendom', but had died suddenly in 1670, probably of peritonitis. Her portrait, presented by Charles II, can still be seen in the Guildhall, and the tragic princess is also depicted in the mural in High Street completed in 1991.

1688 WILLIAM OF ORANGE

Charles II was succeeded by his brother James II. James was an unpopular monarch due to his public adoption of Catholicism which proved unacceptable to Parliament and the majority of the people. The Duke of Monmouth was the first to attempt to remove him but the Western Rebellion of 1685 ended disastrously at the Battle of Sedgemoor. The King's retribution was swift. Monmouth was beheaded and hundreds of his rebel followers were condemned to death by Judge Jefferys' Bloody Assize.

Disquiet grew when James married his second wife the Italian Catholic, Mary of Modena, on 10 June 1688. Within days an invitation was sent by a group of prominent people, known as the Immortal Seven, and which included the Earl of Devon and the Bishop of London, to Prince William of Orange in Holland inviting him to invade England. William, a grandson of Charles I was married to Princess Mary, the daughter of James II. The invitation assured William of military support should he undertake to invade England under the Protestant banner.

That autumn, with 50 ships and 30,000 men, William sailed for England. He evaded James' fleet, but instead of heading north for Hull and York, he turned down Channel and landed at Brixham on 5 November. Once his army was ashore William made his way in land via Newton Abbot.

William's first priority was to establish himself at Exeter where he could assess the support for his cause. He was proceeded into the city by one of his officers, Captain Hicks, and a troop of cavalry.

Hicks found large numbers of men waiting to enlist under the Prince's Protestant banner, but the city leaders were extremely cautious. The Mayor promptly had Hicks arrested when he refused to say under whose authority he was acting. But the crowd that had gathered prevented the Captain from being taken away, so he remained at the Guildhall guarded by two constables.

Later Lord Mordaunt and Dr. Burnett, the Prince's chaplain, reached Exeter but found the West Gate shut. They commanded the Porter to open it and to keep it open on pain of death. Once inside the city walls they demanded the release of Captain Hicks and ordered the mayor and magistrates to welcome the Prince of Orange on his arrival and govern the city for him. The mayor refused saying that he had already sworn allegiance to the King. In the meantime the Bishop and the Dean had moved several miles from Exeter, but the canons of the cathedral had remained behind. More and more of the Prince's troops poured into Exeter and the next day, Friday 9 November, the Prince of Orange himself arrived from Powderham Castle on a white charger and accompanied by the rest of his army.

The Prince took up residence in the Deanery, and after taking some refreshment moved across to the Cathedral where a solemn service was held. William sat in the Bishop's Throne, but the canons did not take their places in the stalls. When Dr. Burnett read the Prince's proclamation and omitted to pray for King James the canons and choir hastily left the Quire. So disappointed was Prince William by the attitude of both the clergy and the civic powers that he threatened to return to his ships and sail back to Holland.

The reluctance of the city to welcome the Prince was doubtless due to recent memories of the Bloody Assize which made those in power extremely wary of changing sides too rapidly. Equally, concern for Exeter's position as England's most prosperous serge market and the possible loss of lucrative business would also have been a factor in the reluctance to switch allegiances too swiftly.

The momentum of William's advance came to a temporary halt, but gradually as an increasing number of influential lords came over to his side, his position strengthened.

The Dean eventually sent word to the Prince begging

forgiveness for having fled the city, and requesting permission to visit him. However the Bishop, Thomas Lamplough, did not return. Instead he fled to King James with news of the invasion, who rewarded him by making him Archbishop of Canterbury.

The Prince of Orange remained in the city, where numerous distinguished Devonians flocked to his standard, until 21 November when he began the march to London. Eventually as his army and advisers turned from him, James abdicated and William and his consort Mary were invited to take the throne in his place. Their coronation was celebrated by Exonians in the traditional way and the conduits once again flowed with wine.

1789 GEORGE III

After so many royal visits occasioned by war the arrival of King George III was effectively the first of the modern era, and not without elements of farce. The King had just recovered from one of his bouts of periodic mental illness and was travelling through the Westcountry in the company of Queen Charlotte and three of their daughters. Charlotte the Princess Royal, Augusta and Elizabeth. The royal party had travelled from Windsor by way of Salisbury and Weymouth. Before reaching Exeter at 7pm on Thursday 13 August 1789 their majesties had paused and taken 'an elegant and sumptuous repast' at Escot, on the Honiton Road. They were met at the bottom of Paris Street by a party of constables and conducted to the site of the Eastgate (the old gateway having been demolished five years earlier) where the Mayor, Jonathan Burnett, the Chamber, and members of the Trade Corporations, in livery, waited to greet them. Two hundred respectable tradesmen had been sworn in as special constables to control the huge crowds estimated as 40,000 strong and crush barriers had been set up in the High Street, where the main drain had been boarded over and gravelled especially for the occasion.

From the Eastgate the procession made its way to the Deanery where the royal party were to stay, while all the church bells rang out in welcome. During the evening the populace celebrated with fireworks and bonfires and the city was fully illuminated. At the

The Cathedral Green. Both William of Orange and George III made the short walk from the Deanery to the Cathedral.

The Bishops Palace.

Modern Eastgate with the Cathedral looming over the rebuilt city centre.

Deanery the Royal party were guarded by the Inniskilling Dragoons who were stationed in the city.

The following morning at 9.45 the Mayor and Chamber were introduced to the King at the Deanery, where the Recorder presented a civic Address, which greatly pleased the Queen. Half an hour later their majesties were escorted across the road to the cathedral where they were greeted at Cloister Gate by the Bishop, John Ross, who conducted them to their seats in the Quire. The King and Queen sat in the Bishop's Throne while the three princesses sat opposite beneath the pulpit. The cathedral was packed for the occasion for as well as the local clergy and civic dignitaries the trade corporations also attended in full livery preceded by their beadles carrying their staffs of office.

After the service the King held a levee at the Bishop's Palace, the first since his illness, and later the Royal party walked in the Bishop's garden and appeared on the terrace where they could be seen by thousands of excited onlookers.

That evening the Chamber had intended to entertain the King to a lavish banquet at the Guildhall but Dean Buller, who it was

Eastgate where George III was greeted by the Mayor and Chamber. The statute on the wall represents Henry VII.

said had conceived the Royal visit as a personal compliment to himself and his wife, had prevented the invitation reaching his majesty. Instead he and the Bishop took the King on a private tour of the cathedral. The Chamber had spent a considerable amount of money, £437*, on preparing the banquet, while Alderman Dennis had personally spent £24 on refurbishing the uniforms of the city band for the occasion.

When the King did not appear at the Guildhall, the enraged Alderman managed to get into the closed cathedral and attempted to confront the King. However Dean Buller spotted his approach and attempted to head him off. A heated argument ensued, with the situation becoming reminiscent of the Barchester Chronicles, but the Dean was adamant and eventually the alderman was ejected by the vergers. The truth of the matter was probably that the King did not wish to set a precedent whereby he had to attend similar banquets at every provincial town he visited.

The next morning the royal party took their leave of the city and continued the tour which next took them to Saltram House near Plymouth. The Royal party spent the night of 27 August at the Deanery on the return journey.

Among those accompanying the King and Queen on their tour was the novelist, Fanny Burney who found Exeter 'close and ugly'. The royal visit was also the subject of a long satirical poem written in Devonshire dialect by Dr. John Wolcot of Kingsbridge who wrote under the pen name of Peter Pindar.

1856 VICTORIA

Queen Victoria never made an official visit to Exeter but nevertheless made two appearances in the city. Her father, Edward, Duke of Kent, was to have had the freedom of the city bestowed on him but died at Sidmouth on 23 January 1820 before the ceremony could take place. The Duke's body was brought to the Royal Clarence Hotel in the Cathedral Close for embalming before being taken back to Windsor for burial.

*Modern equivalent £40,000 approximately.

The young Victoria passed through Exeter on 7 August 1833. She and the Duchess of Kent, her mother, were attended by the Mayor, Henry Blackwell, and the Corporation while they sat in their carriage outside the London Inn. This famous coaching inn stood at the top of High Street near the present Dillons bookshop.

The railway had reached Exeter in 1844 so when the Queen passed through Exeter again on 15 August 1856, it was by train en route from Plymouth to Osborne House on the Isle of Wight. On this occasion the platform of St. David's Station was carpeted and decorated with a profusion of flowers and flags. The Queen, who seems not to have alighted from the train, was presented with nosegays of flowers, as well as fruit and other refreshments by the Mayor, Thomas Norris, and the council, while to the Town Clerk fell the honour of presenting Her Majesty with an address which she graciously received.

Several other notable 'royals' came to Exeter during the nineteenth century. On 16 August 1845 Queen Adelaide, widow of William IV, made a short visit, while on 30 September 1853 His Royal Highness the Duke of Cambridge inspected troops at the Higher or Cavalry Barracks.

On 2 October 1856 the Prince of Wales, later King Edward VII, made an informal visit accompanied by the Hon. Col. Cavendish and his tutor Mr. Gibbs.

The Prince was in Exeter again briefly on 15 November 1860. He was returning from a successful tour of North America and had landed at Plymouth earlier that morning. The Prince's train stopped at St. David's Station where he and his entourage took lunch in the refreshment rooms and inspected a guard of honour provided by the 1st Exeter Rifle Volunteers before resuming his journey.

Prince Arthur, Duke of Connaught, Queen Victoria's third son, paid an incognito visit to Exeter in the spring of 1862. He arrived at Exmouth in the 'Vivid', one of the Royal Yachts, on Tuesday 6 May and the next morning caught the 6.50am train to Exeter where he enjoyed breakfast at Pratt's New London Hotel, before going by carriage to Dunsford and Fingle Bridge. Back in the city he later visited Northernhay, the Castle and the Guildhall before finally attending evensong in the Cathedral after which the

Vergers showed him around the ancient building. Following another meal at the London Inn the Prince returned by train to Exmouth where a crowd had gathered to see him. From the station a cab took the Royal party back to the beach where one of the Vivid's boats was waiting.

The Duke of Connaught proved to be a regular visitor to East Devon. He eventually retired to Sidmouth where he died in January 1942.

1863 saw another private royal visit, this time from the Duke of Cambridge, the Queen's cousin. The Duke arrived on Thursday 2 May and the next morning attended the Good Friday service at the Cathedral where his presence went unnoticed by the majority of the congregation. Among the Duke's party was Sir Richard Airey, the quartermaster general of the army, who had on Lord Raglan's instruction pencilled the order which instigated the Charge of the Light Brigade at the Battle of Balaclava nine years before.

After the service the Duke toured the Cathedral before walking across to inspect the Guildhall. By the time he arrived at its doors the word had got around that a distinguished visitor was in town. At the Guildhall the Duke was recognised by one of the Mace Sergeants and also by a councillor, Mr. Down, who had seen him in the Cathedral and followed the Duke across. In the absence of the Mayor, Down offered to give the Duke an impromptu tour and this offer was accepted. After viewing the civic regalia the Duke expressed his admiration for the portrait of Princess Henrietta. Not surprisingly as the Duke was the Commander-in-Chief of the army the Royal party also visited the Cavalry Barracks and Topsham Barracks before travelling on to Plymouth.

1915 GEORGE V

The grim realities of the First World War brought King George V and Queen Mary to Exeter on 8 September 1915. The royal couple had made two previous visits to the city. The first was on 19 July 1899 when as Duke and Duchess of Edinburgh they had opened an extension to the Royal Albert Memorial College in

67

The Duke and Duchess of Edinburgh arrive outside the Cathedral, July 1899.

Gandy Street, the forerunner of the University, and the 'Victoria' wing of the Royal Devon and Exeter Hospital then in Southernhay. It was as a result of that visit that the hospital got its royal prefix. They also made the almost obligatory visit to the Guildhall and Cathedral.

In 1909 as the Prince and Princess of Wales they made a brief visit whilst on Duchy of Cornwall business.

The 1915 visit was the first official visit by a reigning monarch for 127 years but due to wartime restrictions the King requested that formalities and ceremony should be kept to a minimum. The purpose of the royal visit was to inspect two military hospitals which had been set up in the West of England Eye Infirmary and the Royal Albert Memorial College hostel, now the Exeter and Devon Arts Centre.

After staying overnight on the Royal Train at Bishop's Lydeard, the King and Queen arrived at St. David's Station on Wednesday 8 September. After a brief reception by the Mayor and civic dignitaries the Royal party travelled into town in four motor cars specially loaned for the occasion by prominent citizens, among them the Bishop of Exeter. This was, of course, the first time that the reigning monarch had been seen in Exeter in a motor car.

Despite the secrecy which surrounded the visit huge crowds had assembled and although no decorations had been put up their majesties were cheered loudly as they drove up St. David's Hill, along Queen Street and into High Street where the procession turned in at Broadgate and slowed down so that the Royal passengers could admire the Cathedral and the King could salute the Dean and members of the Chapter who stood before the Deanery. The procession continued down Palace Gate and around to Magdalen Street where patients and nurses from the Royal Devon and Exeter Hospital had come out to watch the King and Queen go by and the 'feeble cheers of the old folk in the Wynards Almshouses were graciously acknowledged'.

The cars pulled into the forecourt of the Eye Infirmary which had become No.1 Hospital and was given over entirely to military wounded. The King, wearing the uniform of a Field Marshall, and Queen toured all the wards and spoke to the patients, then outside in the gardens inspected 170 convalescing soldiers who had been brought in from outlying districts.

The King made a short speech before returning to his car. The procession moved off again, via Magdalen Road, Denmark Road, the Barnfield, Bedford Street and High Street before turning into the narrow confines of Castle Street and No.5 Hospital.

Among the patients here the King met Private G. Bidgood of the King's Own Scottish Borderers to whom he presented the DCM; Private Bidgood having defended a trench single-handed against the enemy overnight in the Dardanelles. After inspecting the hospital and addressing another group of convalescents, the King and Queen returned to the station where the royal train waited to take them further west.

To celebrate this occasion some 800 to 900 wounded soldiers were entertained in the Victoria Hall. Following lunch the soldiers enjoyed a concert provided by the band of the City of Exeter Regiment, A.V.F. The soldiers had been brought into Exeter in 200 cars provided by members of the Automobile Association.

69

1936 EDWARD VIII

Edward VIII's visit to Exeter on 3 June 1936 was probably the briefest of them all. He was driven through the city without stopping on his way from Bradninch to visit Duchy estates in Cornwall. The Mayor, Alderman Gayton, met the King at Whipton and preceded His Majesty the 3½ miles through the city to Pocombe Bridge. The streets were lined with children from all the city's schools who gave the popular young King a rousing welcome.

The King had made two previous visits to the city as Prince of Wales. During the first, on Whit Monday, 16 May 1921, he had unveiled the County War Memorial on the Cathedral Green.

The Prince was on a tour of the Westcountry and arrived in the Cathedral Yard where some 2,000 soldiers were paraded along with representatives of local organisations including the Boy Scouts and the Girl Guides. After unveiling the Memorial which had been designed by Sir Edwin Lutyens, the famous architect, the Prince sealed into the monument a roll of honour bearing the names of 11,601 Devonians who had lost their lives in the Great War. The names were inscribed on a vellum scroll which was placed inside a copper container.

The Prince had especially asked to meet the 250 wounded ex-servicemen on parade, and before returning to the Guildhall, also spoke to Colonel Walcott, a veteran of the Crimea, who was on parade in his bath chair. Also present was Corporal Theodore Veale VC from Dartmouth. His Royal Highness had hoped to visit the Cathedral but lack of time prevented this.

The Prince of Wales was to return to Exeter in June 1927 when as President of the University College of the South West he lay the foundation stone of the Washington Singer building on the new campus site and also opened the new road which was to bear his name.

Six months later Edward VIII had abdicated and gone to France where he married Mrs. Simpson.

During the first half of the twentieth century Exeter received visits from numerous royal personages. Apart from those already mentioned the Prince and Princess of Teck came in 1908, King Gustav of Sweden in 1923, Prince Takamatsu of Japan in March

1931, Princess Catherine of Greece in 1932, and Princess Frederik of Brunswick, granddaughter of the Kaiser in 1934. Other members of the British royal family included Princess Helena Victoria, George Duke of Kent. Queen Mary visited the Guildhall, Cathedral and Hope Hall in 1938 while the Princess Royal inspected a county parade of the Red Cross at St. James Park in 1939. In 1940 the Duke of Kent came to visit some of the 4,000 evacuees who had been sent to Exeter.

1942 GEORGE VI

The abdication of Edward VIII brought George VI to the throne. A quiet, shy man with a speech difficulty he had not been prepared for kingship. However, he and Queen Elizabeth were to find a warm place in the hearts of Exonians.

They were first seen in the city on Wednesday 16 November 1927 when as the Duke and Duchess of York they came to open the new Crippled Childrens' Hospital. They had travelled from London on the Atlantic Coast Express and left the train at Sidmouth Junction to drive across East Devon to Bicton where they were guests of Lord and Lady Clinton.

The next morning the Duke and Duchess drove to Exeter in Lord Clinton's open Armstrong Siddeley tourer via Clyst St. Mary and Heavitree where the car turned into Barrack Road and down to the new hospital at Buckerell Bore. The Duchess opened the main door with a golden key and then was taken to see the Princess Elizabeth Cot, which had been named after her own baby daughter. After touring the hospital, which shortly afterwards would be renamed the Princess Elizabeth Orthopaedic Hospital, the Royal visitors moved on to the Guildhall for luncheon.

Their next engagement was in Pennsylvania where the Duchess opened a new extension of Hope Hall of residence for women at the University College, before driving along Prince of Wales Road towards St. David's Station from where they returned to London by train.

The abdication crisis had heightened interest in the monarchy so when King George passed through Exeter aboard the Royal

71

Train late at night on 1 December 1937 the event attracted considerable local attention. On a dark and stormy night a large crowd gathered on the platform of St. David's Station. Headed by locomotive number 4082 Windsor Castle the royal train glided through the station but the blinds at the carriage windows were drawn and there was no sign of the King.

In May 1942 Exeter attracted the unwelcome attention of the Luftwaffe. 48 hours after the Nazi bombers had left the city centre a smouldering ruin King George VI and Queen Elizabeth came to Exeter to offer sympathy and encouragement to the people as they had done at so many places during the Blitz. It was a visit totally without ceremony and the King and Queen went to parts of Exeter where Royalty had not been seen before. They stopped twice on their tour of the city, in Okehampton Street opposite Emmanuel Church, and at the Triangle, at the bottom of badly hit Paris Street. At both places the people crowded around to welcome their majesties. No royal visit to Exeter would

George VI is presented with the royal sword by Mayor at St. David's Station, July 1950. (Express & Echo)

A thousand years on. The King, Queen and Princess Margaret sit beneath the statutes of Edward the Confessor and Queen Editha during the Cathedral service, July 1950. (Express & Echo)

73

The King and Queen leave the Cathedral accompanied by the Bishop of
Exeter, Doctor Robert Mortimer. (Express & Echo)

be complete without the Guildhall and the Cathedral. The frontage
of the former was protected by a high wall of sand bags to protect
if from blast while the latter was still strewn with rubble following a direct hit on one of the side chapels. The King and Queen
were shown the destruction and the King picked up a lump of
shrapnel which he suggested could be turned back into armaments.

Their majesties were able to see the Cathedral restored to its
former glory when on Monday 10 July 1950 accompanied by
Princess Margaret they attended a service to mark the 900th
anniversary of the transference of the Diocese from Crediton to
Exeter. The Royal party's arrival at St. David's Station that wet
and windy Monday afternoon was heralded by a 21 gun salute
fired by the 296 Field Regiment RA (Royal Devon Yeomanry) in
Northernhay. After receiving the sword from the Mayor, Alderman
J.G.R. Orchard, the King, Queen and Princess drove via St.
David's Hill, New North Road and London Inn Square to High
Street before turning into Broadgate and down to the West Door

74

of the Cathedral where they were welcomed by the Bishop of Exeter, Dr. Robert Mortimer, and the Dean and Chapter. A fanfare of trumpeters of the Household Cavalry announced their entry into the Cathedral where they attended Evensong. Immediately afterwards the Royal party were driven to the Guildhall where they were introduced to the civic dignitaries and shown the city redevelopment plan.

Although it was still drizzling with rain when the time came to leave the King instructed that the roof of the Royal car be lowered so that the huge crowds would get a better view of the occupants on the return drive to the station. But no sooner had the procession moved off than the clouds cleared and the sun shone through.

Sadly King George died on 6 February 1952, but Queen Elizabeth the Queen Mother, made several later visits to Exeter en route to other engagements, and returned to the Cathedral in 1969 when on Tuesday 15 July she attended a celebration of commemoration for Bishop Grandisson who died in 1369. The Archbishop of Canterbury, Dr. Michael Ramsey, preached at the service.

1956 ELIZABETH II

The present Queen has been a more prolific visitor to Exeter than any of her illustrious predecessors. Since her accession in February 1952 Queen Elizabeth II has received Henry VII's sword from four different Mayors of Exeter.

As Princess Elizabeth, she made her first visit to the city in November 1946 when a two day visit took in an inspection of cadet organisations at Topsham Barracks, as well as tours of the Orthopaedic Hospital, which bears her name, and St. Loyes College.

Her Royal Highness returned to Exeter on Friday 21 October 1949 to launch the rebuilding of the bombed city centre. The Princess arrived by car from Bradninch and was greeted at the city boundary by the Mayor, Major General W.G. Michelmore, before driving through Whipton to the Guildhall along roads lined with cheering people. As it was market day, town and country had come together to welcome the Princess and many had stood through heavy showers of rain to ensure they saw the Royal visitor.

Her Majesty Queen Elizabeth II.

After luncheon at the Guildhall the Princess walked in procession to the devastated Bedford Street area where, with a silver plated screwdriver, she gave the final turn to screws securing a bronze plaque, which recorded the start of the rebuilding programme. This took place on the site of a new pedestrian way which was to be named Princesshay, and the outline of the planned way was marked off with white poles draped in bunting.

From Bedford Street the Princess was driven to the new Stoke Hill housing estate where she laid the foundation stone of Toronto House, a new development of 14 dwellings and communal amenities for the aged who had lost their homes in the Blitz. Also present here was the Canadian High Commissioner Mr L. Dana Wilgress. The name Toronto House had been chosen in recognition of the Canadian city's generosity in donating over £500,000 towards the Lord Mayor of London's National Air Raid Distress Fund.

The Princess then visited the new homes of Mrs. Doreen Potter, Mrs. Elizabeth Venner, and Mr. and Mrs. William Rowe, all of

76

whom had been bombed out of their previous houses, in some cases twice, and had now been relocated on the new estate.

From Stoke Hill Princess Elizabeth went to the Cathedral for the first time. Here she was shown around by Bishop Mortimer and Dean Carpenter. After listening to music from the Minstrel's Gallery, the Princess was shown the restoration work nearing completion in the Quire and also watched workmen reassembling the fourteenth century Bishop's Throne which had previously been dismantled and taken to a place of safety for the duration of the war.

After tea at the Guildhall Princess Elizabeth left by car taking her leave of the city at Alphington Cross.

1956 saw the first visit to Exeter by a reigning Queen. This was an important visit not just for the city but also for the University. On Tuesday 8 May Queen Elizabeth II accompanied by her consort Prince Philip, Duke of Edinburgh, arrived by car at Cowley Bridge from Castle Hill, Filleigh, where they had been staying with the Earl and Countess Fortescue. The sword was presented

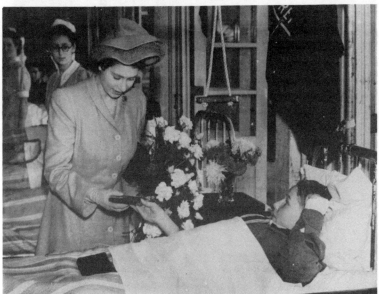

Princess Elizabeth makes her first visit to the Orthopaedic Hospital, 1946.
(Express & Echo)

Princess Elizabeth arrives at the Guildhall, 1949. (Freddie Collins)

The naming ceremony at Princesshay. (Express & Echo)

The Cathedral forms a background as the procession returns to Guildhall.
(Express & Echo)

79

Princesshay today.

Toronto House.

80

by the Mayor, Councillor J.G.J. Greenslade, and the Royal couple were driven on to the campus where the Queen, having been greeted by the Chancellor, the Duchess of Devonshire, handed over the Royal Charter founding the new University of Exeter. She then unveiled the foundation stone of the Faculty of Arts before visiting the Roborough Library.

Lunch at the Guildhall was followed by the opening of the King George V Playing Fields at Countess Wear where 5,000 school children were waiting. Here the Queen formally unlocked the memorial gates before being driven through the ranks of assembled school children. The Royal couple bid farewell to the Mayor at the Bridge Road entrance to the playing fields before leaving for Torquay.

The Royal drive from the Guildhall to Countess Wear holds personal memories. My class from Mount Radford School stood along Barrack Road and waved as the Queen and Duke drove past.

The next major Royal visit came in 1977 as part of the Queen's Golden Jubilee. On the morning of Friday 5 August Her Majesty the Queen and Prince Philip left the Royal Yacht Britannia which was anchored in Torbay and were driven to Exeter coming into the city via Alphington Road, Exe Bridge and Fore Street before arriving at the Guildhall where Roger Keast became the second Mayor to present the sword to Her Majesty. After a brief visit to the Guildhall the Queen and the Duke were driven to the grounds of County Hall where 5,000 people awaited them on a specially laid out walk about route. 1,400 members of Devon youth organisations were among the vast crowd and the youngsters were delighted when they were spoken to by the Royal visitors. After lunch in Bellair, the elegant house which stands in the centre of the grounds, the Queen and the Duke stepped back into their open backed Rolls Royce for the return journey to Torquay.

Two years later they were back in Exeter again. The Queen and Prince Philip arrived at St. David's Station on 9 November 1979 where they were greeted by Sir Richard Hull, the Lord Lieutenant of Devon and the Mayor, Richard van Oppen naturally holding Henry VII's sword. The crowd, gathered outside the station, had waited in the cold but gave the Royal visitors a warm welcome.

This visit gave the Queen the opportunity to return to St. Loyes

81

The Queen receives the sword from the Mayor at the start of the Silver Jubilee visit, 1977. (Express & Echo)

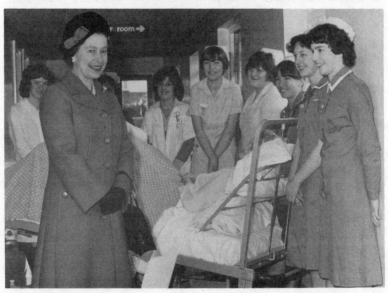

The Queen revisits the P.E.O.H. in 1979. (Express & Echo)

College and the Princess Elizabeth Orthopaedic Hospital after thirty years. At St. Loyes the Queen opened the new Northcote House before touring the training departments and the school of occupational therapy. The Queen was presented with a handbag by Mr. Ted Olek, the foreman of the leather workshop.

Having moved on to the P.E.O.H. the Queen was shown a picture of herself as a little girl, before going on to meet patients and staff, and inspecting the hydro therapy pool and the physio-therapy department.

The next stop was at the Guildhall for lunch where the Mayor pointed out that the tablecloth had been made in Exeter's twin city of Rennes in Brittany. He also explained that the silver bowl of red roses decorating the table were a reminder that in the sixteenth century Queen Elizabeth I had granted the Manor of Topsham to one Peter Smith for a nominal rent of one rose per annum.

The scene outside the Cathedral after the Royal Maundy Service, 1983.
(Express & Echo)

During the afternoon the Queen and Prince Philip toured the Sowton Industrial Estate. Among the premises that they visited was that of Stephen F. Robertson, a firm of saddlers who presented Her Majesty with gifts of a stable rug and a horse's head collar.

The Royal visitors left from Exeter Airport in a twin engined Andover of the Queen's Flight.

The Queen's next visit to Exeter on 31 March 1983 was to be unique in the city's history for Her Majesty had come to distribute the Royal Maundy at the Cathedral.

The tradition of the Royal Maundy goes back over 700 years and is an ancient ceremony based on Christ's action the night before the crucifixion in which he washed the feet of his disciples. The name Maundy comes from Mandatum, a commandment, following the words of St John's Gospel, 'I have given you an example, that you should do as I have done to you'.

In medieval times the monarch personally washed the feet of old people. This ended with the reign of William III. Since then the monarch has made gifts of money instead. The recipients in 1983 received two leather purses; a red one which contained a £5 note and a 50p coin, and white one containing the actual Maundy money, four small coins of 1p, 2p, 3p and 4p denominations. The set of four have a legal tender of just 10p but together they are of great value to collectors. To those who receive them from the sovereign, the tiny coins are priceless.

The Queen and the Duke of Edinburgh arrived at St David's where the Mayor, Mrs Pat Spencer, was on hand with the sword. From the station the Royal couple were driven through cheering crowds to Broadgate where Bishop Eric Mercer was waiting to meet them at the top of the new processional way. Boys from the Cathedral School lined the Way holding yellow wreaths proclaiming VIVAT E II. The West front of the Cathedral, freshly cleaned, had been stripped of its long standing scaffolding, and the bells rang out as, for the first time in its long history, a reigning Queen of England entered the ancient building.

Inside seated in the Nave facing the centre aisle 114 Devonians, 57 men and 57 women, representing each year of the sovereign's age, waited to receive the Royal Maundy.

The procession through the building to the Quire included the uniquely colourful sight of the Queen's bodyguard, the Yeoman of the Guard.

After the Duke of Edinburgh had read the first lesson from the Nave pulpit, the first of the Maundy gifts were distributed. The Queen, followed by the Royal Almoner, the Bishop of Rochester, Rt Rev David Say, and his assistants, who wore the traditional linen towels used since 1883, made the presentations of purses to those on the South side of the Cathedral. This was followed after the second lesson by those on the North side. During the distributions the choirs of the Cathedral and the Chapels Royal sang anthems including Handel's stirring coronation piece 'Zadok the Priest'.

After the glories of the service, which was broadcast live on BBC Radio 4, the Royal couple posed for group photographs outside the Cathedral before moving on to a reception in the Bishop's Palace followed by lunch at the Guildhall. Meanwhile the delighted recipients enjoyed a cup of coffee and a biscuit in the Chapter House whilst excitedly recalling the highlights of the service. Among the recipients were two with Cathedral connections. Mr Gerry Dawson was formerly a verger while Mr Jack Brown had been a member of the Voluntary Choir for over 60 years.

During the afternoon the Queen and the Duke of Edinburgh undertook a walkabout in the High Street before leaving the city. The Queen apparently enjoyed the occasion so much that she allowed the schedule to be extended by some 45 minutes.

During the reign of Queen Elizabeth II Exeter has enjoyed more Royal visits than at any other time in its history. Besides Her Majesty the Queen and the Duke of Edinburgh, Exeter has also enjoyed a number of other official Royal visits, many of which have been connected with the long term redevelopment of the city.

In 1974 the Duke of Gloucester officially opened the new Royal Devon and Exeter Hospital at Wonford, while Princess Alexandra visited the 1983 Devon County Show at the Whipton showground and was at the Guide Dog Centre at Cleve House, Exwick on 5 May 1988. The Duchess of Gloucester visited Franklyn House in

Prince Phillip pauses in the High Street to assist Emily Maguire over the barrier during the Royal walkabout, 1983. (Express & Echo)

The Duchess of Kent visits the Royal Devon and Exeter Hospital, Southernhay (now Dean Clarke House) in December 1956. (Freddie Collins)

Princess Alexandra in a procession to the Cathedral during a visit to Exeter in the fifties. (Freddie Collins)

Carefully does it. The Prince of Wales climbs the scaffolding to inspect restoration work on the West front of the Cathedral, 1978. (Express & Echo)

St. Thomas on 7 October 1982, and the Duchess of Kent opened both the Clifton Hill Sports Centre and the Exeter and Devon Arts Centre on 13 March 1985; The Arts Centre being the same building which the Duke and Duchess of Edinburgh had first opened back in 1899 as the Royal Albert Memorial College, the forerunner of Exeter University.

His Royal Highness, the Prince of Wales has been a frequent visitor to Exeter in recent years where he has taken a particular interest in preserving aspects of the Cathedral. In 1978 a group of Women's Institute members going into the Cathedral for an evening tour were amazed to meet the Prince as he left the building after a secret meeting with the Dean and Chapter. As a result of that meeting Prince Charles agreed to become the President of the Cathedral's Preservation Trust and the next summer returned to make an official visit. On 13 July 1979 the Prince attended a service at the Cathedral at which it was announced that he was also to become the first Patron of the Friends of the Cathedral. Afterwards the Prince went out to inspect the progress of the preservation work and climbed a forty foot ladder to meet the masons and watch them at work high on the West Front. Whilst putting on a safety helmet before making his climb the Prince managed to hit his head on some scaffolding, which prompted the

Prince Charles meets Trevor Conway, the Head Boy of the Cathedral School, 1978.

89

Lord Lieutenant, Sir Richard Hull, to point out that it was Friday the thirteenth.

Prince Charles also went to see the stonemasons working in their yard before walking through crowds to St. George's Hall where he met appeal helpers at a reception. From the reception the Prince walked back to the Cathedral where he presided over a business meeting before having lunch at the Deanery with the Dean, Clifford Chapman, after which he was driven to Wyvern Barracks from where he departed by helicopter.

Following the success of the Restoration Appeal the Prince returned to Exeter on Thursday 12 November 1987 to launch the Cathedral's Music Foundation Trust Appeal. This sought to raise £1 million to ensure the long term future of the Cathedral Choir. After attending evensong at which he read the second lesson Prince Charles talked to members of the Choir in the Vestry before going down to the Chapter House to meet 120 specially invited guests. On his way to the Chapter House the Prince stopped to inquire about the workings of the Cathedral's amplification system from the operator, Brian Matthews. Brian has taken many of the photographs for this book.

An equally frequent Exeter visitor has been Princess Anne, the Princess Royal. In October 1983 Princess Anne made two visits in three days while touring the Westcountry. The first was almost called off when fog threatened to prevent the Princess's Andover aircraft from landing at Exeter Airport. Fortunately all was well and she duly arrived at a packed Cathedral where she was to attend a special concert in aid of the St. John Ambulance. This involved a 300 strong choir drawn from local Middle Schools and St. John cadets, backed by the Devon County Youth Orchestra. The Cathedral Choir and Royal Marine trumpeters also took part, and the highlight of the concert was a rendition of Prokofiev's Peter and the Wolf in which broadcaster Richard Baker took the role of the narrator. Afterwards Princess Anne met both local and St. John Ambulance dignitaries at a reception held at County Hall.

Forty eight hours later the Princess drove back into Exeter at the wheel of her own Rover car. She was received at the Guildhall by the Mayor, Ray 'Spider' Long, before going on to the University

Great Hall for another gala concert, this time in aid of the Save the Children Fund. Included in the programme was a special Save the Children anthem composed by Mr Victor Whitburn of the University School of Education.

In 1985 Princess Anne was back at the University on a flying visit to open the British Veterinary Association Annual Congress which that year also incorporated the Fourth European Congress. The Princess landed on the University sports field in a Wessex helicopter of the Queen's Flight at 10am on 12 September. In the conference hall Princess Anne officially opened the Congress before touring the commercial stands, and in the afternoon she listened to a lecture on the work of the BVA overseas. The animal connection continued at her next engagement which was a visit to the Donkey Sanctuary and Slade Riding for the Disabled Centre at Sidmouth.

The Princess flew into Exeter yet again, two years later, when on 9 October 1987 her Wessex helicopter landed in the grounds of St. Loyes College of Occupational Therapy. Princess Anne dug the first turf for a new O.T. teaching block, and then spent the next three hours meeting students and trainees at the College before opening a £90,000 extension to the commercial skills training department. Among the students the Princess met were three from the USA on an exchange visit, Jeanette Nazarcian, Kareen Duverlie and Lynne Dinsdale who were thrilled to meet a real British Royal.

To complete the visit Princess Anne presented diplomas to Occupational Therapy students at a graduation ceremony which was also attended by Sir Steuart Pringle of the Royal Marines who had been badly injured in an IRA bomb attack.

From St. Loyes the Princess was driven on to the Royal Devon and Exeter Hospital at Wonford where she made a special visit to the Intensive Care Unit. Due to the frail nature of the patients the Princess spoke to them in private. Having recently become the new patron of the Intensive Care Society of Great Britain, Princess Anne spent five hours talking to nursing staff as well as former patients. From the hospital the Princess was driven to the Middlemoor Headquarters of the Devon and Cornwall Police where she was picked up by helicopter.

Another extremely popular visitor has been the Princess of Wales. Princess Diana made her first appearance in Exeter on Wednesday 2 July 1986, when she was welcomed by thousands of cheering people. Having arrived at Exeter Airport in an Andover of the Queen's Flight the Princess made an impromptu walk about before being driven into the city where her first engagement was at the new £8 million Plaza Leisure Centre in St. Thomas. Here after being presented with a bouquet by six year old Jodie Hall, Princess Diana was invited to press a button which brought the pool area to life, including the much talked about water flume slide. Within moments of it being switched on, dozens of children were sliding down the twisting flume into the pool below.

The Princess inspected all aspects of the Plaza including the Bodyline health and fitness club, the squash courts and the sports hall before trying her hand at snooker in the Mainframe clubroom.

The Princess of Wales tries her hand at snooker during her visit to the Plaza Leisure Centre in 1986. (Express & Echo)

From the Plaza the Princess was driven to the Guildhall where she enjoyed a buffet lunch of local salmon, turkey salad and strawberries and cream. Then it was time to step outside on to the saluting base to watch a pageant depicting 150 years of the police service in Exeter. The parade also included the fire and ambulance services and featured tableaux depicting Sherlock Holmes and Dr Watson as well as escaped Dartmoor prisoners.

The police were not only in the parade. Security throughout the entire visit was extremely tight, with plain clothes officers mingling with the crowds while armed officers from the firearms squad were also on duty. This did not deter Princess Diana from making another walk about in the High Street before returning to the airport.

The Princess of Wales' second visit to Exeter was on Wednesday 26 September 1990, when after a variety of engagements around the county she rounded off the day at the City's Relate Centre where couples with relationship problems can receive counselling. The Princess was welcomed outside the ancient Wynards building by the Mayor, George Clark, and showed her knowledge of Relate's work by joining in a debate during a counsellor training session.

Princess Diana's visit again highlighted the degree of security which now surrounds Royal occasions. Shortly before the Princess's arrival a sniffer dog undertaking a routine search started to bark indicating that it had found something. In fact the dog had unearthed a stale meat pie which had been discarded near the well in the centre of the cobbled Wynards courtyard. Royal visits have come a long way since the Britons' queen stopped the battle between Arviragus and Vespasian in AD 49.

Happily royalty continue to be frequent visitors to this 'Ancient and Loyal City'. Even as this book was going to press Prince Charles was back in Exeter. On Tuesday 19 November 1991 the Prince returned to the cathedral to attend a special evensong in celebration of the Music Foundation. Earlier in the afternoon the Prince had opened the new NFU offices at Pines Hill.

Royalty from afar was also in Exeter that month. The King of Tonga paid a private visit to the city in order to inspect a new personal aeroplane at the airport.

For nearly two thousand years kings, queens, princes and princesses have come to Exeter in time of war, rebellion and unrest. In modern times royal visits have been happy occasions and it is to be hoped that Henry VII's sword will be presented to many more monarchs in the years to come.

The Queen and Prince Phillip enjoy a joke with the Mayor, Mrs. Pat Spencer, at the Guildhall 1983.